POETIC JUSTICE

The funniest, meanest things ever said about lawyers

Edited by Jonathan & Andrew Roth

NOLO PRESS•950 PARKER ST, BERKELEY, CA 94710

PRINTING HISTORY

FIRST EDITION	February 1988
ILLUSTRATIONS	Linda Allison
BOOK DESIGN & LAYOUT	Toni Ihara
	Jackie Clark
PRINTING	Delta Lithograph

Library of Congress Catalog Card Number: 87-063575

ISBN 0-87337-072-4

DEDICATION

To our father and mother, and our brother the lawyer
(who did not inspire this book).

CONTENTS

INTRODUCTION

We did not begin this book with any evil intent towards lawyers. Initially, we envisioned it as a useful and hopefully entertaining collection of thoughts and writings about that profession. As our store of quotations grew, however, a definite pattern emerged without our conscious will or effort. In the course of our research, it became ever clearer that down through the centuries of written history and literature, as well as in the oral folk-tales, proverbs and curses of every culture in the world, the lawyer has been universally hated.

Primitive humanity lived in a state of nature —without the benefit of legal counsel. Then, as life became more complex, mankind crowded into walled cities, breeding lice and lawyers. Writing brought writs, law introduced legalities and lawyers invented fees. The hoary forebears of today's attorneys were despised by the Babylonians and Assyrians, distrusted by the Egyptians and the Hittites, and loathed by the Phoenicians and Hebrews. It is no wonder that the wise philosophers of the ancient Greeks, the greatest minds that Western Civilization has produced, detested lawyers. Likewise the greatest minds of Eastern Civilization. Even Jesus, who suffered the worst sinners, tax collectors and adulterers to come unto him, drew the line at attorneys.

There are those who feel that corruption or lead poisoning led to the fall of the Roman Empire. It is our opinion that after four hundred years of Roman Law, the inhabitants welcomed the barbarians. During the Dark and Middle Ages, both nobleman and peasant felt that the only good lawyer was a hanged lawyer.

The Renaissance attempted to enlighten humanity with ideas of justice and equality. Unfortunately, in attempting to bring Europe under the Rule of Law, they succeeded only in subjecting it to the Rule of Lawyers.

In the eighteenth and nineteenth centuries, revolution after revolution attempted to overthrow this tyranny of lawyers, often thinly disguised by

figure-head monarchs. Inevitably, though, after the dust had settled, the legislatures and parliaments filled up with those same fell attorneys.

Naturally, as we surveyed this vast and ancient stream of invective we occasionally found a positive sentiment towards the attorney. At first we were puzzled by this seeming anomaly: however, after eliminating those quotations that were clearly textually corrupt, or mistranslated, and those made by vicious criminals released through legal technicalities to prey on yet more innocent victims or by appreciative landlords who had been assisted in their exploitation of widows and orphans, we discovered that the only ones with good words for the legal profession were invariably either lawyers or their mothers.

Modern science has been unable to determine whether it is the naturally twisted and vicious soul which is drawn, by some sinister sympathy, into the practice of law, or if the study of that black science is responsible for corrupting an initially innocent spirit. This question is interesting, but in the final analysis it is irrelevant to this work, for we are concerned only with the final product of legal education: the consenting adult of sound mind and body, the reasonable man or woman, who, willfully, and with malice aforethought, becomes a lawyer.

Why, then, does the human race love to hate lawyers? What is it that is so patently offensive about attorneys?

One possible explanation is their extraordinary love of money. The courtroom — the stage on which the injury and pain of so many people is revealed, is a mere profit center for the attorney. It is not the righting of a wrong that motivates the lawyer, but rather the writing of a check.

Another reason might be their disregard for truth and common sense. While all the peoples of the earth hold honesty a virtue and lying a sin, the race of lawyers consider an over-attention to truth to be a professional weakness. They are sculptors of the truth, molding and twisting reality, twirling fact on a potter's wheel of rhetoric and sophism, until truth itself is malformed to the lawyer's satisfaction, convenience and profit.

Or it may be a lack of scruples. Indeed, for the lawyer there is no commandment so sacred that it cannot by scoured for loopholes, no taboo so dreadful that it cannot be appealed on a technicality, no tactic or argument so offensive that it cannot be blithely tossed to a jury, and no human emotion so noble that it cannot be sacrificed on the altar of advantage. The lawyer is a mercenary in the war between good and evil. The expression "legal ethics" is an oxymoron.

Perhaps the lawyer's intentional obfuscation is the cause. As a matter of course, instead of uncovering the plain facts of a dispute, the legal cabal enshrouds them in sheets and reams of ambiguity. The language of the law is incomprehensible, its procedures inscrutable, its results all too often unfathomable.

Could it be that it is the lawyer's banality which mankind finds so offensive? For the legal mind, all the struggles of mankind, the bold enterprises and the spiritual quests, love and hate and striving, are reduced to torts and briefs and a big, fat fee. The lawyer is the least romantic of human beings.

Perhaps, then, it is that they simply do not do what they are supposed to do. We may not like doctors, but at least they doctor. Bankers are not very popular but at least they bank. Policemen police and undertakers take under. But lawyers do not give us law. We receive not "the gladsome light of jurisprudence," but rather precedents, objections, appeals, stays, filings and forms, motions and counter-motions, all at $250 an hour.

None of these vices, not their greed, nor their lying, their unscrupulousness, their obfuscation, their banality, not even their clannishness, nor their boorishness, nor their haughtiness, nor even all of these taken together, quite explains the world's timeless loathing of lawyers. We must admit that we are at a loss to provide a single good reason why the lawyer is so unpopular. We offer, therefore, the hundreds of good reasons that follow.

Jonathan Roth
Andrew Roth
New York, November 1987

PART ONE

THE NATURE OF THE LEGAL BEAST

Shyster lawyers—a set of turkey buzzards whose touch is pollution and whose breath is pestilence.

—*G. G. Foster*

❖

Shyster. 1. A crooked conniving small-time lawyer. 2. Any lawyer.

—*Dictionary of American Slang*

❖

Lawyers are jackals.

—*Erasmus*

❖

I think we may class the lawyer in the natural history of monsters.

—*John Keats*

❖

...lawyers as a group—a great, obfuscating, overbloated throng—make me buggy.

—*Andrew Tobias*

❖

It is a strange trade, that of advocacy. Your intellect, your highest heavenly gift, hung up in the shop window like a loaded pistol for sale, will either blow out a pestilent scoundrel's brains, or the scoundrel's salutary sheriff's officer's (in a sense), as you please to choose for your guinea.

—*Thomas Carlyle*

❖

Lawyers are monsters, demons, when they smirk at each other when a trial ends…when they let lose at each other with the strawfire of their rhetorical arguments with their artificial emotion and superficial indignation, when they cry paid-crocodile tears or discover clever sophisms and questionable evasions and wretched chicanery, when they laugh at the confusion of a matter, rejoice over the sensationalism of a case, mutter with a pack of thieves, unmoved by the human suffering facing them, as soon as it ceases to be their case, enchanted with the sound of their own phraseology.

—*Cornelius Veth*

❖

Shyster: A term of contempt for an unscrupulous, tricky, mean person often applied to lawyers.

—Dictionary of Americanisms

❖

A thorough-paced Lawyer eyes what he calls a curious question with the same sort of instinctive glee as a Lecher does a fresh grisette from the country, or a Quin Epicure a Haunch of Venison.

—Jeremy Bentham

❖

Any profession that suffers from so foul a reputation must, in some way, provoke it.

—Alan Dershowitz

❖

Lawyers are always more ready to get a man into troubles than out of them.

—Oliver Goldsmith

❖

I know you lawyers can with ease
Twist words and meanings as you please;
That language, by your skill made pliant,
Will bend to favor every client.

—John Gay

❖

To succeed in the trades, capacity must be shown; in the law, concealment of it will do.

—Mark Twain

❖

[The lawyer has] a professional obligation to place obstacles in the path of truth.

—Monroe Freedman

❖

The worthy administrators of justice are like a cat set to take care of a cheese, lest it should be gnawed by the mice. One bite of the cat does more damage than twenty mice can do.

—Voltaire

❖

A lawyer is a liar with a permit to practice.
                    —Anonymous
                         ❖

Never was any item so openly sold as the perfidy of lawyers.
                    —Tacitus
                         ❖

A good lawyer is a great liar.
                    —Edward Ward
                         ❖

Lawyering is within the relatively narrow category of occupations where borderline dishonesty is fairly lucrative.
                    —Eric Schnapper
                         ❖

Lawyers fall more into the category of politicians, civil servants and jockeys— some of them are probably honest, but how can you be sure?
                    —Lloyd Cutler
                         ❖

Lawyers are just like physicians; what one says the other contradicts.
                    —*Sholem Aleichem*
                           ❖

He's a wonderful talker who has the art of telling you nothing in a great harangue.
                       —*Moliere*
                           ❖

Come, you of the law, who can talk, if you please
Till the man in the moon will allow it's a cheese.
                    —*Oliver Wendell Holmes*
                           ❖

What's the first excellence in a lawyer? Tautology. What's the second? Tautology. What's the third? Tautology.
                    —*Richard Steele*
                           ❖

If you think that you can think about a thing, inextricably attached to something else, without thinking of the thing it is attached to, then you have a legal mind.
—*Thomas Reed Powell*

❖

Some men are heterosexual, and some are bisexual, and some men don't think about sex at all...they become lawyers.
—*Woody Allen*

❖

...those modern purveyors of streamlined voodoo and chromium-plated theology, the lawyers.
—*Fred Rodell*

❖

Poetic justice: a lawyer with his tongue cut out.
—*Anonymous*

❖

A lawyer: one skilled in circumvention of the law.
—*Ambrose Bierce*

❖

"A conscience for hire," as our peasants call lawyers.
—*Dostoevsky*

❖

He is no lawyer who cannot take two sides.
—*Charles Lamb*

❖

We will not at present inquire whether the doctrine which is held on this subject
by English lawyers be or be not agreeable to reason and morality,—whether it be
right that a man should, with a wig on his head and a band round his neck, do
for a guinea what, without those appendages, he would think it wicked and
infamous to do for an empire,—whether it be right that, not merely believing but
knowing a statement to be true, he should do all that can be done, by sophistry,
by rhetoric, by solemn asseveration, by indignant exclamation, by gesture, by
play of features, by terrifying one honest witness, by perplexing another, to cause
a jury to think that statement false.
—*Thomas Babington Macaulay*

❖

Pettifogger: A little dirty attorney, ready to undertake any litigious or bad cause.
—*Captain Francis Grose*

❖

Trafficking in the mad wrangles of the noisy court, he lets out for hire his anger and his speech.
—*Seneca*

❖

"Men that hire out their words and anger," that are more or less passionate according as they are paid for it, and allow their client a quantity of wrath proportionate to the fee which they receive from him.
—*Joseph Addison*

❖

I said there was a society of men among us, bred up from their youth in the art of proving by words multiplied for the purpose, that white is black, and black is white, according as they are paid. To this society all the rest of the people are slaves.
—*Jonathan Swift.*

❖

With books and money placed for show,
Like nest eggs, to make clients lay,
And for his false opinions pay.

> —*Samuel Butler*

❖

You get a reasonable doubt for a reasonable price.

> —*Criminal attorneys' saying*

❖

The lawyer is a gentleman who rescues your estate from your enemies—and keeps it to himself.

> —*Henry Peter Brougham*

❖

Where there is a rift in the lute, the business of the lawyer is to widen the rift and gather the loot.

> —*Arthur G. Hayes*

❖

Being a lawyer is like being a bottle of ketchup in a restaurant that specializes in bad steaks. It covers a multitude of sins.

—Jerome Weidman

❖

Those lawyers with Hah-Vud accents are always thinking up new ways to take advantage of people.

—Harry Truman

❖

A lawyer is someone who helps you get what's coming to him.

—Anonymous

❖

A lawyer is someone who defends your interest, and takes the principal.

—John Stringer

❖

A lawyer is a man who profits by your experience.

—Anonymous

❖

[A lawyer] defends you at the risk of your pocketbook, reputation and life.
                                   —*Eugene E. Brussell*
                                        ❖

Lawyer: a fellow who is willing to go out and spend your last cent to prove he's right.
                                   —*Anonymous*
                                        ❖

I always figured that being a good robber was like being a good lawyer.
                                   —*Willie Sutton*
                                        ❖

Lawyers help those who help themselves.
                                   —*Anonymous*
                                        ❖

Lawyers earn their bread in the sweat of their browbeating.
                                   —*James Huneker*
                                        ❖

Doctors purge the stomach, parsons purge the soul, lawyers purge the purse.
                        —*German proverb*
                               ❖

Lawyers ain't like coachmen, they take their tip before they start.
                        —*American proverb*
                               ❖

A learned class of very ignorant men.
                             —*Erasmus*
                               ❖

I am not so afraid of lawyers as I used to be. They are lambs in wolves' clothing.
                   —*Edna St. Vincent Millay*
                               ❖

There may be said to be three sorts of lawyers: able, unable, and lamentable.
                     —*Robert Smith Surtees*
                               ❖

Our colleagues in medicine...at least use cadavers for their practice efforts.... We cut our trial teeth on real live clients.

—*F. Lee Bailey*

❖

What is the difference between a barrister and a solicitor? Merely the difference between a crocodile and an alligator.

—*Punch*

❖

There are two kinds of lawyers: those who know the law and those who know the judge.

—Anonymous

❖

PART TWO
THE GLADSOME LIGHT OF JURISPRUDENCE

The law is a sort of hocus-pocus science, that smiles in yer face while it picks yer pocket; and the glorious uncertainty of it is of more use to the professors than the justice of it.

—*Charles Macklin*

❖

Laws are made to be broken so that lawyers may drive Daimlers and drink Mumm's.

—*A. P. Herbert*

❖

Possession is nine points of the law and lawyers fees are the other ninety-one points.

—*Anonymous*

❖

In law, nothing is certain except the expense.

—*Samuel Butler*

❖

Law is a shrewd pickpurse.

—James Howell

❖

I think the law is really a humbug and a benefit principally to lawyers.

—Henry David Thoreau

❖

I decided law was the exact opposite of sex; even when it was good, it was lousy.

—Mortimer Zuckerman

❖

If the laws could speak for themselves, they would complain of the lawyers.

—George Saville

❖

Solicitor to client: "You have an excellent case, Mr. Peabody, how much justice can you afford?"

—Punch

❖

Justice oft leans to the side where your purse hangs.
—*Danish proverb*

❖

Poetic Justice, with her lifted scale,
Where, in nice balance, truth with gold she weighs
And solid pudding, against empty praise.
—*Alexander Pope*

❖

Laws go where dollars please.
—*Portuguese proverb*

❖

Law is like a flag, and gold is the wind which makes it wave.
—*Russian proverb*

❖

People say law but they mean wealth.
—*Ralph Waldo Emerson*

❖

Of course there's a different law for the rich and the poor; otherwise, who would go into business?
—*E. Ralph Stewart*

❖

The law has a nose of wax, one may turn it as one pleases.
—*German proverb*

❖

Lawyers use the law as shoemakers use leather; rubbing it, pressing it, and stretching it with their teeth, all to the end of making it fit their purposes.
—*Louis XII of France*

❖

No written law can be so plain, so pure
But wit may gloss and malice may obscure.
—*John Dryden*

❖

Law is often a triumph over equity and good conscience.
—*Jesse Hoyt*

❖

Imagine the appeals
Dissents and remandments
If lawyers had written
The Ten Commandments.
>   —*Harry Bender*
>   ❖

Justice is always the aim of the law—but only, I think, on a theoretical level.
>   —*F. Lee Bailey*
>   ❖

Justice has been described as a lady who has been subject to so many miscarriages as to cast serious reflections upon her virtue.
>   —*William Prosser*
>   ❖

This is a court of law, young man, not a court of justice.
>   —*Oliver Wendell Holmes, Jr.*
>   ❖

In the Halls of Justice the only justice is in the halls.
                         —*Lenny Bruce*
                              ❖

Justice is incidental to law and order.
                         —*J. Edgar Hoover*
                              ❖

Equal justice under law often means unequal justice under lawyers.
                         —*Jerold S. Auerbach*
                              ❖

As a very young lawyer, from books that I read
I thought justice and law were the same;
But I soon put that juvenile thought from my head
And I studied the rules of the game.
                         —*Joe Swan*
                              ❖

Law is but a heathen word for power.
                         —*Daniel Defoe*
                              ❖

The law doth punish man or woman
That steals the goose from off the common
But lets the greater felon loose
That steals the common from the goose.

—Anonymous

❖

Law licks up all.

—Scottish proverb

❖

Law is only a fancy name
For all injustice the world contains.

—Franz Grillparzer

❖

This home of opportunity where every man is the equal of every other man
before the law if he isn't careful.

—Finley Peter Dunne

❖

Justice is what we get when the decision is in our favor.
—John W. Raper

❖

An ounce of favor is worth a pound of law.
—French proverb

❖

Screw the law—you get the guy off any way you can.
—William Kuntsler

❖

Talent whips truth every time.
—Judge Don B. Morgan

❖

The law is a business whose outlook is shared by its major clients.
—Laura Nader

❖

If war is too important to be left to the generals, surely justice is too important to be left to lawyers.

—Robert McKay

❖

Law is a bottomless pit, it is a cormorant, a harpy, that devours everything.

—John Arbuthnot

❖

Law guards us from all evils but itself.

—Henry Fielding

❖

Hell and Chancery are always open.

—Folk saying

❖

Law is one of the arts—black arts!

—Douglas William Jerrold

❖

[The law] is a bum profession.
                    —*Clarence Darrow*
                            ❖

There is no worse torture than the torture of Lawes.
                    —*Francis Bacon*
                            ❖

Laws and rights are inherited like a perpetual disease.
                    —*Goethe*
                            ❖

No man can imagine, not Swift himself, things more shameful, absurd and grotesque than the things which do take place daily in the law.
                    —*Sir Arthur Helps*
                            ❖

The United States is the greatest law factory the world has ever known.
                    —*Charles Evan Hughes*
                            ❖

The law is a dull dog.
                                        —*Charles Dickens*
                                ❖

If you laid all of our laws end to end, there would be no end.
                                        —*Mark Twain*
                                ❖

In the old days there was one law for the rich and one for the poor; nowadays there are millions of laws for everybody.
                                        —*Anonymous*
                                ❖

The more mandates and laws which are enacted, the more there will be thieves and robbers.
                                        —*Lao-Tzu*
                                ❖

Law makes more knaves than it hangs.
                                        —*Samuel Butler*
                                ❖

It usually takes a hundred years to make a law, and then, after it has done its work, it usually takes a hundred years to get rid of it.
—*Henry Ward Beecher*
❖

American legal practice is now on its own legs, and careth not a damn for either English precedent or common sense.
—*H. L. Mencken*
❖

"If the law supposes that," said Mr. Bumble..., "the law is a ass, a idiot."
—*Charles Dickens*
❖

The law is a hard queer thing. I do not understand it.
—*Poundmaker (Cree Chief)*
❖

Do not waste your time looking up the law in advance, because you can find some Federal district court that will sustain any proposition you make.
—*Sam Ervin*
❖

Many words have a legal meaning. Others have a legal meaning very unlike their ordinary meaning. For example, the word "daffy-down-dilly." Ha! Yes, I advise you never to do such a thing. No, I certainly advise you *never* to do it.
—*Dorothy Sayers*

❖

Ignorance, superstition, the price of princes, the interests of legislators, caprice, fantasy—these are the sources of the great body of the law.
—*Anatole France*

❖

Law has been called a bottomless pit, not so much because of its depth, as that its windings are so obscure nobody can see the end.
—*George P. Morris*

❖

Master, master, come quick! Here's a fish caught up in the net like a working man's rights in the law.
—*Shakespeare*

❖

Lawyers: persons who write a 10,000 word document and call it a brief.
—*Franz Kafka*

❖

...no segment of the English language in use today is so muddy, so confusing, so hard to pin down to its supposed meaning, as the language of the Law. It ranges only from the ambiguous to the completely incomprehensible.
—*Fred Rodell*

❖

As a collection our statute books might be summed up as beyond the average citizen's pocket to purchase, beyond his bookshelves to accomodate, beyond his leisure to study and beyond his intellect to comprehend.
—*Sir Cecil Carr*

❖

To say that lawyers have no interest in the uncertainty of the law is to say that glaziers have no interest in the breaking of windows.
—*Laurence Gronlund*

❖

The more you allow the courts to clarify things the worse you make them.
—Henry Bourassa

❖

When lawyers talk about the law, the normal human being begins to think of something else.
—Richard Ingrams

❖

PART THREE
NOT NECESSARILY THE WORLD'S MOST POPULAR PROFESSIONAL

The first thing we do, let's kill all the lawyers.
                    —*Shakespeare*
                         ❖

The renowned Peter the Great, being at Westminster Hall in term time, and
seeing multitudes of people swarming about the courts of law, is said to have
inquired what all those busy people were, and what they were about, and, being
told that they were lawyers, replied "Lawyers! Why, I have but four in my whole
kingdom, and I design to hang two of them as soon as I get home."
                    —*William S. Walsh*
                         ❖

Why is there always a secret singing
When a lawyer cashes in?
Why does a hearse horse snicker
Hauling a lawyer away?
                    —*Carl Sandburg*
                         ❖

Yes, Jamie, he was a bad man, but he might have been worse; he was an Irishman, but he might have been a Scotchman; he was a priest, but he might have been a lawyer.

—Samuel Parr

❖

I would be loth to speak ill of any person who I do not know deserves it, but I am afraid he is an attorney.

—Samuel Johnson

❖

A lawyer art though? Draw not nigh!
Go carry to some fitter place
The keenness of that practised eye,
The hardness of that sallow face.

—William Wordsworth

❖

The lawyer-class is the most mischievous of all classes, the one that most clogs the wheels of progress.

—Laurence Gronlund

❖

When there are too many policemen, there can be no liberty;
When there are too many soldiers, there can be no peace;
When there are too many lawyers, there can be no justice.
—Lin Yutang
❖

That one hundred and fifty lawyers should do business together ought not to be expected.
—Thomas Jefferson (referring to the U.S. Congress)
❖

When God wanted to chastise mankind he invented lawyers.
—Russian proverb
❖

Love all men—except lawyers.
—Irish proverb
❖

May your life be filled with lawyers.
—Mexican curse
❖

Most lawyers are swine. And not even nice swine.
—*Charles McCabe*

❖

God save us from a lawyer's *et cetera*.
—*French proverb*

❖

A client twist his attorney and counselor is like a goose twixt two foxes.
—*James Howell*

❖

I had rather that my daughter should be burned at the stake than to have to suffer what I have gone through with lawyers.
—*Hetty Green*

❖

"Virtue in the middle," said the Devil, as he sat down between two lawyers.
—*Danish proverb*

❖

It is better to be a mouse in the mouth of a cat than a man in the hands of a lawyer.
>   —*Spanish proverb*
>   ❖

I wouldn't write a song about any of them.
>   —*John Lennon*
>   ❖

I, Lucius Titus, have written this my testament without any lawyer, following my own natural reason rather than excessive and miserable diligence.
>   —*The will of a citizen of Rome*
>   ❖

St. Yves is from Brittany
A lawyer but not a thief
Such a thing is beyond belief!
>   —*English rhyme*
>   ❖

God works wonders now and then;
Behold! a lawyer an honest man.

—Ben Franklin

❖

"An Honest Lawyer"—book just out—
What can the author have to say?
Reprint perhaps of ancient tomb—
A work of fiction anyway.

—Grace Hibbard

❖

I question not but there are many attorneys born with open and honest hearts:
but I know one that has had the least practice who is not selfish, trickish and
disingenuous.

—William Shenstone

❖

Personally, I don't think you make a lawyer honest by an act of legislature. You've got to work on his conscience. And his lack of conscience is what makes him a lawyer.

—Will Rogers
❖

I used to be a lawyer, but now I am a reformed character.
—Woodrow Wilson
❖

Apologists for the profession contend that lawyers are as honest as other men, but that is not very encouraging.
—Ferdinand Lundberg
❖

Bar associations are notoriously reluctant to disbar or even suspend a member unless he has murdered a judge downtown at high noon, in the presence of the entire committee on Ethical Practices.
—Sydney J. Harris
❖

For a while you worried that a rich man with a cunning lawyer could no longer get ahead in this country. But the Great American Dream is not moribund. Anyone who labors industriously and thinks deviously can go anyplace he chooses....That's why we have the Bill of Rights. Also the American Bar Association.

—*Art Spander*

❖

There's no better way of exercising the imagination than the study of the law. No poet ever interpreted nature as freely as a lawyer interprets truth.

—*Jean Giraudoux*

❖

In the heels of the higgling lawyers,
Too many slippery if and buts and however,
Too much hereinbefore provided whereas,
Too many doors to go in and out of.
When the lawyers are through
What is there left, Bob?
Can a mouse nibble at it
And find enough to fasten a tooth in?

—*Carl Sandburg*

❖

Among other amiable weaknesses, lawyers have this one, of commencing to sum up a case by telling the jury that the merits of a cause lie in a nutshell and then going on to argue for hours to prove it.

—*C. Nestelle Bovee*

❖

Lawyers have been known to wrest from reluctant juries triumphant verdicts of acquittal for their clients, even when those clients, as often happens, were clearly and unmistakably innocent.

—*Oscar Wilde*

❖

The lawyer is your friend because
He guides you through the maze of laws.
In fact we write them round about
So only we can make them out.

—*Mayor Moore*

❖

They do tricks even I can't figure out.
—*Harry Houdini*

❖

It is hard to say whether the doctors of law or of divinity have made the greatest advances in the lucrative business of mystery.
—*Samuel Goldwyn*

❖

He explained things to me. Sort of. The way lawyers do.
—*Craig Vetter*

❖

For a good time, hire a hooker,
For a lot of time, hire my attorney.
—*Anonymous prison cell graffiti*

❖

They have no lawyers among them, for they consider them as a sort of people whose profession it is to disguise matters.
—*Sir Thomas More*

❖

If it weren't for the lawyers we wouldn't need them.
                    —*William Jennings Bryan*
                              ❖

King Ferdinand Wisely provided that no lawyers could join in the new colonies sent to America, lest law suits should get a footing in the new world.
                    —*Michel de Montaigne*
                              ❖

A Spanish conquistador-governor is said to have implored the king of Spain to send no lawyers to his new domains: "They are all devils."
                    —*Charles M. Haar*
                              ❖

Shall we nourish individuals in the community merely to take the advantage of our distresses, and under pretence of doing us justice, demand any proportion of our property they may think fit? In a few years we may expect their influence to be so great, that no man will be able to apply to the laws without mortgaging a certain part of his estate to a lawyer.
                    —*Benjamin Austin*
                              ❖

Woe unto ye also, ye lawyers! for ye lade men with burdens grievous to be born, and ye yourselves touch not the burdens with one of your fingers.

—*Jesus*

❖

A more sickening task cannot well be undertaken, than a perusal of the two vast volumes of "Laws of Prince Edward Island" numbering 1,719 pages: the great curse of the Island has been a plethora of laws and lawyers, the little village or capital, Charlottetown, having for its share a legal confederacy aptly designated "the forty thieves."

—*B.W.A. Sleigh*

❖

As through this world I've travelled,
I've seen lots of funny men;
Some will rob you with a six gun
And some with a fountain pen.

—*Woody Guthrie*

❖

A lawyer with his briefcase can steal more than a hundred men with guns.
                                    —*Mario Puzo*
                                        ❖

The legal trade, in short, is nothing but a high-class racket.
                                    —*Fred Rodell*
                                        ❖

Between grand theft and a legal fee,
There only stands a law degree.
                                    —*Anonymous*
                                        ❖

Your pettifoggers damn their souls
To share with knaves in cheating fools.
                                    —*Robert Butler*
                                        ❖

By law's dark by-ways he had stored his mind
With wicked knowledge how to cheat mankind.
                                    —*George Crabbe*
                                        ❖

Here malice, rapine, accident conspire,
And now a rabble rages, now a fire;
Their ambush here relentless ruffians lay,
And here the fell attorney prowls for prey.
                              —*Samuel Johnson*
                        ❖

A man may as well open an oyster without a knife as a lawyer's mouth without
a fee.
                              —*Barten Holyday*
                        ❖

A lawyer's ink writes nothing until you have thrown silver into it.
                              —*Estonian proverb*
                        ❖

Law is the second oldest profession.
                              —*Anonymous*
                        ❖

A man without money needs no more fear a crowd of lawyers than a crowd of
pickpockets.

—*William Wycherly*

❖

A fox may steal your hens, Sir,
A trull your health and pence, Sir,
Your daughter may rob your chest, Sir,
Your wife may steal your rest, Sir,
A thief your goods and plate.

But this is all but picking,
With rest, pence, chest and chicken;
It ever was decreed, Sir,
If Lawyer's hand is fee'd, Sir,
He steals your whole estate.

—*John Gay*

❖

The lawyer who practices law as an art, is sure to entrap and ensnare; he will hold you with one hand and rifle your pockets with the other.
                                        —*Joseph Bartlett*
                                        ❖

Ninety percent of our lawyers serve 10 percent of our people. We are over-lawyered and under-represented.
                                        —*Jimmy Carter*
                                        ❖

People know instinctively something which honest lawyers dare not contemplate. The fact is that the law simply does not work, not for the average person. The law may in some circumstances and under some conditions work for government bureaucracies and giant corporations, but the average guy knows he is never going to get anything out of it but grief. This helps to explain why people see lawyers as professional buzzards who prey upon people's troubles. It also helps to explain why lawyers tend to be such a joyless lot who often have trouble keeping even their own self-respect. Lawyers may often do well, but not often by doing good. . .even when they try.
                                        —*Charles E. Sherman*
                                        ❖

We may well be on our way to a society overrun by hordes of lawyers, hungry as locusts, and brigades of judges in numbers never before contemplated.
—*Warren Burger*

❖

Three Philadelphia lawyers are a match for the Devil.
—*New England proverb*

❖

He saw a lawyer killing a viper
On a dunghill hard by his own stable
And the Devil smiled, for it put him in mind
Of Cain and his brother Abel.
—*Samuel Coleridge*

❖

What chance has the ignorant, uncultivated liar against an educated expert?
What chance have I...against a lawyer?
—*Mark Twain*

❖

Here lies John Shaw,
Attorney-at-law;
And when he died,
The Devil cried,
Give us your paw,
John Shaw,
Attorney-at-law!

—H.J. Learing

❖

The Devil makes his Christmas pie of lawyer's tongues.
—English proverb

❖

No lawyer will ever go to Heaven as long as there is room for more in Hell.
—French proverb

❖

Thus 'tis we say
though quite uncivil,
A cunning lawyer
beats the devil!

  —*Early American rhyme*

❖

Lawyer and liar are synonymous terms.

  —*Edward Cooke*

❖

Lawyers sometimes tell the truth—they will do anything to win a case.

  —*Anonymous*

❖

In all points out of [the lawyers'] own trade they were the most ignorant and
stupid generation among us, the most despicable in common knowledge,
avowed enemies to all knowledge and learning, and equally disposed to pervert
the general reason of mankind in every other subject of discourse as in that of
their own profession.

  —*Jonathan Swift*

❖

Necessity knows no law; I know some attorneys of the same.
—*Ben Franklin*

❖

He who pleads his own cause may have a fool for a client; but it's more probable that he who employs a lawyer will have a knave for an attorney.
—*Edward Parsons Day*

❖

To some lawyers all facts are created equal.
—*Felix Frankfurter*

❖

Anyone can end up a lawyer if he fucks up enough.
—*Jerry Della Femina*

❖

The local courthouse is a haven for vagrants sleeping in the corridors, incompetent lawyers and bail bondsmen swarming like vultures, and hack political appointees clothed in the robes of justice destroying lives through prejudice, whim, and limited legal ability.
—*Leonard Downie, Jr.*

❖

Sometimes a man who deserves to be looked down upon because he is a fool is despised only because he is a lawyer.
                              —*Montesquieu*
                                ❖

Lawyers and insurance agents deserve one another.
                              —*Craig Vetter*
                                ❖

Doctors take the Hippocratic Oath;
Lawyers take the oath of hypocrisy.

                    The law is a bright light
                    which blinds all reasonable men.

                                        She offered her honer
                                        He honored her offer.
                                        And all night long
                                        It was honor and offer.

        —*Graffiti off the walls at Boalt Hall School of Law*
                                ❖

PART FOUR
THE MALPRACTICE OF LAW

Bluster, sputter, question, cavil; but be sure that your argument be intricate enough to confound the court.

                             —William Wycherly

❖

When you have no basis for an argument, abuse the plaintiff.

                             —Cicero

❖

Among attorneys in Tennessee the saying is: When you have the facts on your side, argue the facts. When you have the law on your side, argue the law. When you have neither, holler.

                             —Albert Gore, Jr.

❖

In law what plea so tainted and corrupt
But, being season'd with a gracious voice,
Obscures the show of evil?

                             —Shakespeare

❖

Truth is stranger than fiction, especially in lawsuits.

—*Anonymous*

❖

My suit has nothing to do with assault or battery, or poisoning, but it is about three goats, which, I complain, have been stolen by my neighbor. This the judge desires to have proved to him but you with swelling words and extravagant gestures, dilate on the Battle of Cannae, the Mithraditic War, and the perjuries of the insensate Carthaginians, the Syllae, the Marii and the Mucii. It is time, Postumus, to say something about my goats.

—*Martial*

❖

Four sheep, a hog and ten bushels of wheat settled an Iowa breach of promise suit where $25,000 damages were demanded. The lawyers got all but the hog, which died before they could drive it away.

—*Item appearing in the Cheyenne Leader*

❖

A jury consists of twelve persons chosen to decide who has the better lawyer.

—*Robert Frost*

❖

Nearly every lawsuit is an insult to the intelligence of both plaintiff and defendant.

—*E.W. Howe*

❖

Law is like a sieve; it is very easy to see through it, but a man must be considerably reduced before he can get through it.

—*Samuel George Morton*

❖

To seek the redress of grievances by going to law, is like sheep running for shelter to a bramble-bush.

—*Louis Weston Dilwyn*

❖

A piece of paper, blown by the wind into a law court may in the end only be drawn out again by two oxen.

—*Chinese proverb*

❖

Law is like a mouse-trap; easy to enter but not easy to get out of.
                              —*Arthur J. Balfour*
                                    ❖

Whoever goes to law, goes into a glass house, where he understands little or nothing of what he is doing; where he sees a small matter blown up into fifty times the size of its intrinsic contents, and through which, if he can perceive any other objects, he perceives them all discolored and distorted.
                              —*Philip Skelton*
                                    ❖

Lawsuit: a machine which you go into as a pig and come out of as a sausage.
                              —*Ambrose Bierce*
                                    ❖

Those who go to law are the birds, the court the field, the judge the net, and the lawyers the fowlers.
                              —*Pope Pius I*
                                    ❖

Litigant: One who fails to realize that the only party who makes money out of litigation is the lawyer.

—*Bennett Cerf*

❖

Lawsuits would tend to increase to a frightening extent if people were not afraid of the tribunals and if they felt confident of always finding in them ready and perfect justice...I desire therefore that those who have recourse to the tribunals should be treated without pity and in such a manner that they shall be disgusted with law and tremble to appear before a magistrate.

—*Chinese Emperor K'ang Hsi*

❖

The epithet *beautiful* is used...by lawyers to describe cases which ruin all the parties to them.

—*G.B. Shaw*

❖

The very definition of a good award is that it gives dissatisfaction to both parties.

—*Goodman v. Sayers*

❖

Court receiver, laughs and thrills
But in the end we just pay those lawyers their bills.
—*George Harrison*

❖

The penalty for laughing in the courtroom is six months in jail. If it were not for this penalty, the jury would never hear the evidence.
—*H.L. Mencken*

❖

Honesty is the best policy, because good lawyers come high.
—*Anonymous*

❖

A happy death is better than a lawsuit.
—*Spanish proverb*

❖

May you have a lawsuit in which you know you are right.
—*Spanish Gypsy curse*

❖

I have never met a litigator who did not think he was winning the case right up
to the moment when the guillotine came down.

—*William Baxter*

❖

Battledore and shuttlecock's a very good game, when you ain't the shuttlecock
and two lawyers the battledores, in which case it gets too excitin' to be pleasant.

—*Charles Dickens*

❖

Do not frequent a law court,
Do not loiter where there is a dispute.

—*Babylonian proverb*

❖

Avoid law suits beyond all things; they influence your conscience, impair your
health and dissipate your property.

—*Jean de la Bruyère*

❖

Discourage litigation. Persuade your neighbors to compromise whenever you can. Point out to them how the nominal winner is often a real loser in fees, expenses and waster of time.

—*Abraham Lincoln*

❖

Never go to law, if you win you lose and if you lose you're lost.

—*Anonymous*

❖

He who is fond of maintaining an action will soon be without the means of maintaining himself.

—*Punch*

❖

The worst thing you can wish someone would be "may you be in litigation the rest of your life." I'd rather someone would kill me.

—*Tom Berenger*

❖

Whene'er a bitter foe attack thee,
Sheathe they sword, thy wrath restrain:
Or else will magistrates and lawyers
Divide thy wealth, they purse retain.
—Samuel Archevolti
❖

Litigant: a person about to give up his skin for the hope of retaining his bones.
—Ambrose Bierce
❖

As a litigant, I should dread a lawsuit beyond almost anything short of sickness
and death.
—Judge Learned Hand
❖

The houses of lawyers are roofed with the skins of litigants.
—Welsh proverb
❖

Lawyer-house built upon fool head.
—Jamaican proverb

❖

A lawsuit is a fruit-tree planted in a lawyer's garden.
—Italian proverb

❖

Lawsuits consume time and money and rest and friends.
—George Herbert

❖

Fond of lawsuits, little wealth; fond of doctors, little health.
—Spanish proverb

❖

The lawyers prayer: God grant that disputes may arise that I may live.
—Spanish proverb

❖

A lawyer's dream of heave —every man reclaimed his property at the resurrection, and each tried to recover it from all his forefathers.

—*Samuel Butler, II*

❖

I seek the kind of verdict where you can hear the angels sing and the register ring.

—*Melvin Belli*

❖

The accused presented the best witnesses that money could buy.

—*Oscar Wilde*

❖

Always remember that when you go into an attorney's office door, you will have to pay for it, first or last.

—*Anthony Trollope*

❖

Little money; little law.

—*Anonymous*

❖

Fees to judges, puisne judges, clerks, protonotaries, philizers, chirographers, underclerks, proclamators, counsel, witnesses, jurymen, marshall, tipstaffs, criers, porters, for enrollings, exemplifications, bails, vouchers, returns, caveats, examinations, filings of words, entries, declarations, replications, recordats, nolle prosequis, certioraris, mittimus, demurrers, special verdicts, informations, scire facias, supersedeas, habeas corpus, coach hire, treating of witnesses, etc.
                    —*John Arbuthnot*
                         ❖

The wrangling Courts, and stubborn law,
To smoke, and crowds, and cities draw;
There selfish Faction rules the day,
And Pride and Avarice throng the way;
Diseases taint the murky air,
And midnight conflagrations glare. . .
                    —*Sir William Blackstone*
                         ❖

The practice of law in most courtrooms today is about as modern as performing surgery in a barber shop.
                    —*Gordon Schaker*
                         ❖

Lawyers on opposite sides of a case are like the two parts of shears; they cut what comes between them, but not each other.

—*Tryon Edwards*

❖

Once (says an Author; where I need not say)
Two Trav'lers found an Oyster in their way;
Both fierce, both hungry; the dispute grew strong,
While Scale in hand Dame Justice pass'd along
Before her each with clamour pleads the Laws.
Explain'd the matter, and would win the cause,
Dame Justice weighing long the doubtful Right
Takes, opens, swallows it, before their sight.
The cause of strife remov'd so rarely well,
"There take" (says Justice), "take ye each a shell.
We thrive at Westminster on Fools like you:
'Twas a fat oyster—live in peace—Adieu."

—*Alexander Pope*

❖

Going to law is losing a cow for the sake of a cat.
—*Chinese proverb*

❖

If no one paid a fee for lawsuits, there would be less of them! As it is, feuds, charges, malevolence and slander are encouraged. For just as a physical illness brings revenue to doctors, so a diseased legal system entices advocates.
——*Gaius Silius*

❖

It isn't the bad lawyers who are screwing up the justice system in this country — it's the good lawyers. . . if you have two competent lawyers on opposite sides, a trial that should take three days could last six months.
—*Art Buchwald*

❖

Suits at court are like winter nights, long and wearisome.
—*Thomas Deloney*

❖

Who goes to law should have three bags: one of papers, one of money, and one of patience.

—*French proverb*

❖

A lawsuit is a fir tree in a lawyer's garden, that takes root and never dies.

—*Italian proverb*

❖

The plaintiff and the defendant in an action at law are like two men ducking their heads in a bucket, and daring each other to remain longest under water.

—*Samuel Johnson*

❖

He that loves law will get his fill of it.

—*Scottish proverb*

❖

Appeal: in law, to put the dice into the box for another throw.

—*Ambrose Bierce*

❖

An appeal is when ye ask one court to show its contempt for another court.
—*Finley Peter Dunne*

❖

You cannot live without lawyers, and certainly you cannot die without them.
—*Joseph H. Choate*

❖

To set an attorney to work to worry and torment another man is a very base act;
to alarm his family as well as himself, while you are sitting quietly at home.
—*William Cobbett*

❖

Now it is possible to see in all the regions of the Orient powerful and rapacious
classes of men flitting from one forum to another, besieging the homes of the
wealthy, and like Spartan or Cretan hounds sagaciously picking up the tracks
until they come to the very lairs of lawsuits.
—*Ammianus Marcellinus*

❖

PART FIVE

JUDGE NOT LEST YE BE JUDGED

I have great respect for the judiciary, as fine a lot of cross and indignant men as ye'll find anywhere.

—*Finley Peter Dunne*

❖

He wastes his tears who weeps before the judge.

—*Italian proverb*

❖

When the judge's mule dies, everybody goes to the funeral; when the judge himself dies, nobody goes.

—*Arabic proverb*

❖

A lifetime of the law alone turns judges into dull, dry husks.

—*William O. Douglas*

❖

I think I'm about as colorful and flamboyant as a cold mashed potato sandwich.

—*Judge Harry E. Claiborne*

❖

A judge is a man who ends a sentence with a sentence.
—*Anonymous*

❖

Judges are best in the beginning; they deteriorate as time passes.
—*Tacitus*

❖

[Judicial] impartiality is an acquired taste, like olives.
—*Simon Rifkind*

❖

Thwackum was for doing justice, and leaving mercy to heaven.
—*Henry Fielding*

❖

There are no more reactionary people in the world than judges.
—*V.I. Lenin*

❖

For the most part, judges are narrow-minded lawyers.
                    —*Philip B. Kurland*
                              ❖

The discretionary power of judges is often little better than the caprice of a tyrant.
                    —*George P. Morris*
                              ❖

The thing to fear is not the law, but the judge.
                    —*Russian proverb*
                              ❖

Every relative generates its correlative. Slaves breed tyrants, imposters are bred by dupes, Ignorant and prejudiced Judges breed disingenuous, shameless, overbearing advocates.
                    —*Jeremy Bentham*
                              ❖

[A judge is] a member of the bar who once knew a governor.
                                                    —*Curtis Bok*
                                                        ❖

Judges...are picked out from the most dextrous lawyers who are grown old or lazy; and having been biased all their lives against truth and equity, lie under such a fatal necessity of favoring fraud, perjury and oppression, that I have known some of them to have refused a large bribe from the side where justice lay, rather than injure the faculty, by doing anything unbecoming their nature or their office.
                                                    —*Jonathan Swift*
                                                        ❖

Lawyers are the only civil delinquents whose judges must of necessity be chosen from themselves.
                                                    —*C.C. Colton*
                                                        ❖

A judge is a law student who marks his own papers.
                                                    —*H.L. Mencken*
                                                        ❖

We have long suffered under base prostitution of law to party passions in one judge, and the imbecility of another.
—*Thomas Jefferson*

❖

Judge: "I have listened to your case Mr. Smith, and I am no wiser now than I was when you started."
F.E. Smith: "Possibly not, My Lord, but far better informed."
—*F.E. Smith*

❖

Judges Know the law, More or less.
—*Michael Millman*

❖

The statute books are exceedingly muddled. I seldom look into them.
—*Judge Mathew B. Begbie*

❖

Starting off [a trial] with a completely open mind is a terribly dangerous thing to do.

—*Sir Melford Stevenson*

❖

Judges are apt to be naif, simple-minded men, and they need something of Mephistopheles.

—*Oliver Wendell Holmes, Jr.*

❖

Judges are the weakest link in our system of justice, and they are also the most protected.

—*Alan Dershowitz*

❖

You give me a lousy judge and the best system and he'll find out how to mess it up.

—*Mario Merola*

❖

The acme of judicial distinction means the ability to look a lawyer straight in the eye for two hours and not hear a damned thing he says.
                              —*Chief Justice John Marshall*
                                            ❖

A judge's duty is to grant justice, but his practice is to delay it; even those judges who know their duty adhere to the general practice.
                              —*Jean de la Bruyère*
                                            ❖

To be a good judge, you must have inestimable good judgment, a sense of fair play and a darn good bladder.
                              —*Mrs. Loyal C. Payne*
                                            ❖

The hungry judges soon the sentence sign,
And wretches hang that jurymen may dine.
                              —*Alexander Pope*
                                            ❖

Tell God the truth, but give the judge money.
—Russian proverb

❖

For gold his sword the hireling ruffian draws,
For gold the hireling judge distorts the laws.
—Samuel Johnson

❖

Judges are but men, all in all ages have shown a fair share of frailty. Alas! Alas!
Judges without convictions are most generous in handing them out.
—Anonymous

❖

The worst crimes of history have been perpetrated under their sanction, the
blood of martyrs and patriots, crying from the ground, summons them to
judgment.
—Charles Sumner

❖

The world has produced fewer instances of truly great judges than it has of great men in almost every other department of civilized life.

—*Horace Binney*

❖

We must remember, too, that we have to make judges out of men, and that by being made judges their prejudices are not diminished and their intelligence is not increased.

—*Robert J. Ingersoll*

❖

Always remember that you were an attorney once. Not too long ago you were out there trying to make a living in the same vineyards. The black robe doesn't change things. You're the same guy as you were back then.

—*Remarks made at a special orientation program for new judges.*

❖

When the court doesn't know, it consults precedent. The court that made the precedent guessed at it. Yesterday's guess, grown gray and wearing a big wig, becomes today's justice.

—*Frank Crane*

❖

Lawful, adj. Compatible with the will of a judge having jurisdiction.
—*Ambrose Bierce*

❖

The Lord Chief Justice of England recently said that the greater part of his judicial time was spent investigating collisions between propelled vehicles, each on its own side of the road, each sounding its horn and each stationary.
—*Philip Guedalla*

❖

Judges, like the criminal classes, have their lighter moments.
—*Oscar Wilde*

❖

PART SIX
THE LAW IS ITS OWN REWARD

I defended about one hundred forty people for murder in this country and I think in all of the cases I received just one Christmas card from all of these defendants.

—*Samuel Leibowitz*

❖

ABOUT THE EDITORS

Andrew Roth is a writer currently working on an anecdotal history of crime in Manhattan. He is a graduate of Occidental College in Los Angeles. Jonathan Roth is a graduate student, at present writing a doctoral dissertation in Roman History at Columbia Univesity. Both were born and raised in Northern California and live in New York City.

INDEX BY AUTHOR

For Your Poetic Justice T-Shirt

POETIC JUSTICE

J.D., Esq.

A lawyer with his tongue cut out.

$10.95 each

Size: ☐ sm.   ☐ med.   ☐ lg.   ☐ x-lg.

Order Form

Quantity		Unit Price	Total

Subtotal_____

___Please send me a catalogue

Tax_____

Tax: (CA only; San Mateo, LA, & Bart Counties, 6 1/2%, Santa Clara 7%, all others, 6%)

Postage & Handling_____

Total_____

Postage & Handling:

No. of Books	Postage & Handling	
1	$1.50	
2-3	$2.00	
4-5	$2.50	Over 5, add 5% of total before tax

Please allow 2-4 weeks for delivery. For faster service, add $1 for UPS delivery (no P.O. boxes, please).

Name_____

Address_____

_____

_____VISA   _____Mastercard

#_____ exp._____

Signature_____

Credit card information or a check may be sent to NOLO Press, 950 Parker Street, Berkeley, CA 94710 or call (415) 549-1976

or

Send a check only to NOLO Distributing, Box 544, Occidental, CA 95465

Phone ( )_____